THE TWELVE DAYS OF CHRISTMAS

YULETIDE CHARACTER PIECES ARRANGED BY PHILLIP KEVEREN

— PIANO LEVEL —
INTERMEDIATE

ISBN 978-1-4950-1843-5

HAL•LEONARD®
CORPORATION

7777 W. BLUEMOUND RD. P.O. BOX 13819 MILWAUKEE, WI 53213

In Australia Contact:
Hal Leonard Australia Pty. Ltd.
4 Lentara Court
Cheltenham, 3192 Victoria, Australia
Email: ausadmin@halleonard.com.au

Visit Hal Leonard Online at
www.halleonard.com

Visit Phillip at
www.phillipkeveren.com

PREFACE

Christmas carols are an essential part of what makes the season magical. These rich songs return to us each year, carrying with them memories of Christmases past – each one a unique and priceless musical jewel.

I have chosen twelve of my favorite tunes for this collection, arranging them to be Yuletide character pieces for the piano. All twelve key signatures are explored, each major key paired with its related minor. Most pianists have keys in which they prefer to play, and keys they would rather avoid. These settings will coax all of us out of our comfort-key zones at some point!

May your Christmases be filled with the joy of music-making.

Sincerely,

Phillip Keveren

BIOGRAPHY

Phillip Keveren, a multi-talented keyboard artist and composer, has composed original works in a variety of genres from piano solo to symphonic orchestra. Mr. Keveren gives frequent concerts and workshops for teachers and their students in the United States, Canada, Europe, and Asia. Mr. Keveren holds a B.M. in composition from California State University Northridge and a M.M. in composition from the University of Southern California.

CONTENTS

JOY TO THE WORLD
C major/A minor

Words by ISAAC WATTS
Music by GEORGE FRIDERIC HANDEL
Adapted by LOWELL MASON
Arranged by Phillip Keveren

O COME, O COME, IMMANUEL

G major/E minor

Plainsong, 13th Century
Words translated by JOHN M. NEALE
and HENRY S. COFFIN
Arranged by Phillip Keveren

GOOD CHRISTIAN MEN, REJOICE

D major/B minor

14th Century Latin Text
Translated by JOHN MASON NEALE
14th Century German Melody
Arranged by Phillip Keveren

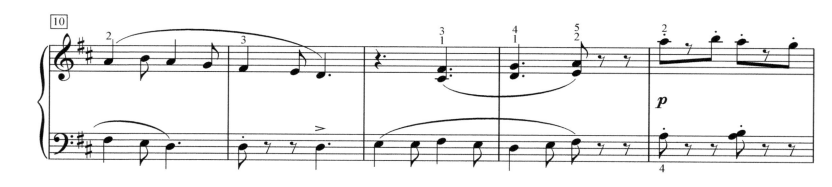

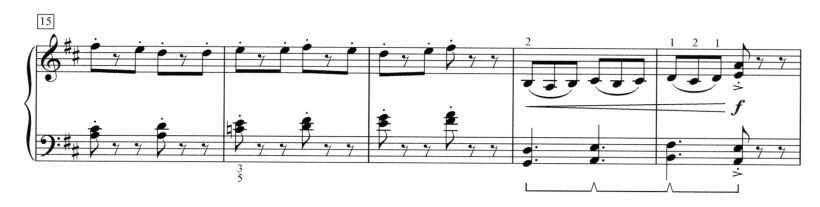

WHAT CHILD IS THIS?

A major/F♯ minor

Words by WILLIAM C. DIX
16th Century English Melody
Arranged by Phillip Keveren

COVENTRY CAROL
B major/G♯ minor

Words by ROBERT CROO
Traditional English Melody
Arranged by Phillip Keveren

ANGELS WE HAVE HEARD ON HIGH

E major/C# minor

Traditional French Carol
Translated by JAMES CHADWICK
Arranged by Phillip Keveren

Moderately, flowing (♩ = 120)

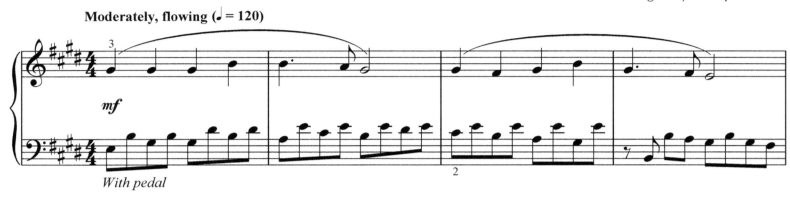

STILL, STILL, STILL

Gb major/Eb minor

Salzburg Melody, c.1819
Traditional Austrian Text
Arranged by Phillip Keveren

WE THREE KINGS OF ORIENT ARE

D♭ major/B♭ minor

Words and Music by
JOHN H. HOPKINS, JR.
Arranged by Phillip Keveren

ANGELS FROM THE REALMS OF GLORY

A♭ major/F minor

Words by JAMES MONTGOMERY
Music by HENRY T. SMART
Arranged by Phillip Keveren

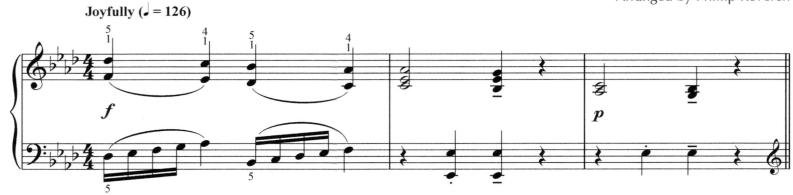

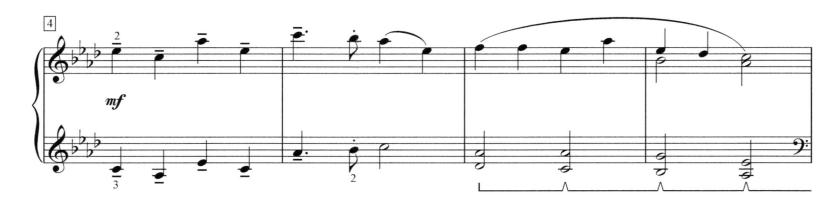

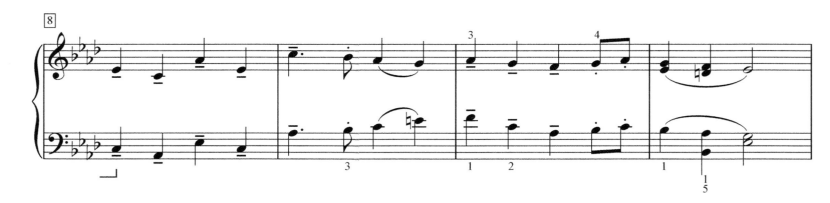

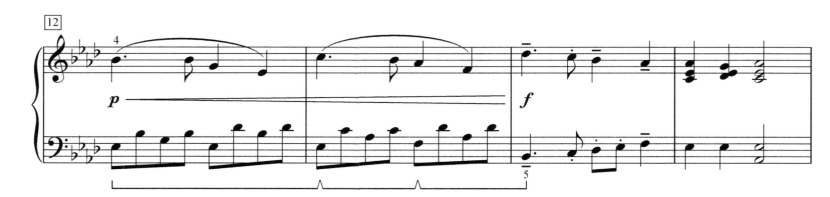

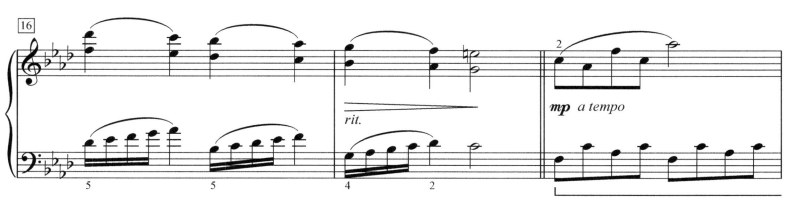

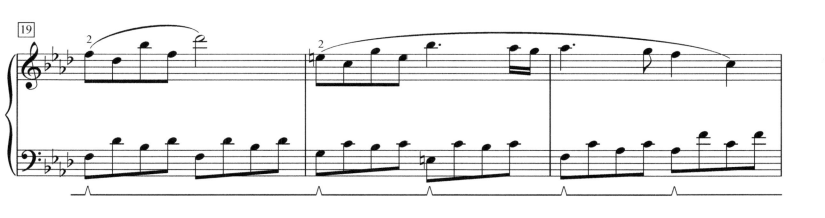

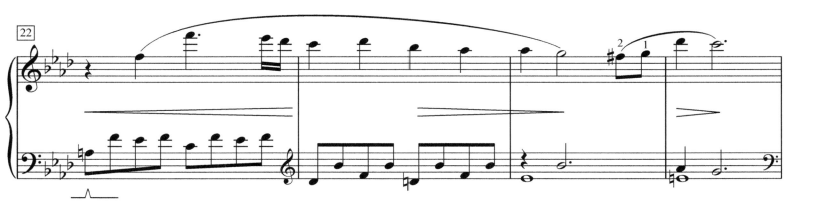

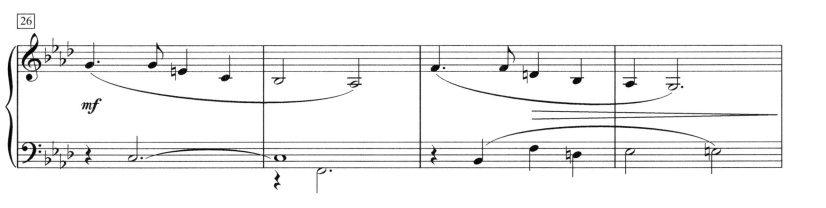

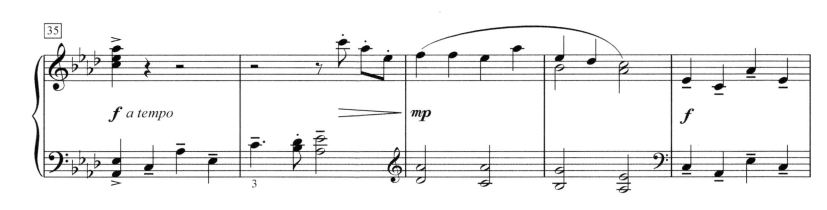

UKRAINIAN BELL CAROL

E♭ major/C minor

Traditional
Arranged by MYKOLA LEONTOVYCH
Arranged by Phillip Keveren

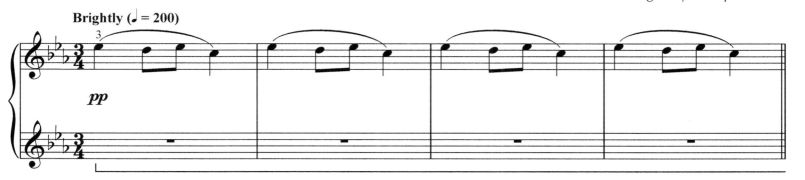

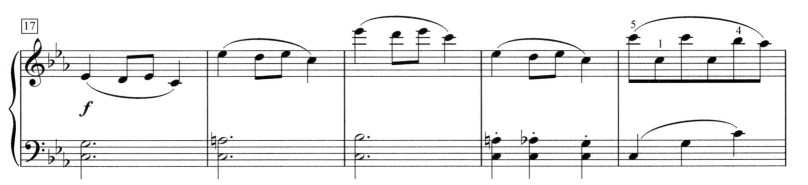

Ringing, with freedom (♩ = 96)

SILENT NIGHT

B♭ major/G minor

Words by JOSEPH MOHR
Translated by JOHN F. YOUNG
Music by FRANZ X. GRUBER
Arranged by Phillip Keveren

O COME, ALL YE FAITHFUL

(Adeste fideles)
F major/D minor

Music by JOHN FRANCIS WADE
Latin Words translated by FREDERICK OAKELEY
Arranged by Phillip Keveren

Stately (♩ = 108)

With pedal

THE PHILLIP KEVEREN SERIES

PIANO SOLO

00156644	**ABBA for Classical Piano**	$15.99
00311024	**Above All**	$12.99
00311348	**Americana**	$12.99
00198473	**Bach Meets Jazz**	$14.99
00313594	**Bacharach and David**	$15.99
00306412	**The Beatles**	$17.99
00312189	**The Beatles for Classical Piano**	$16.99
00275876	**The Beatles – Recital Suites**	$19.99
00312546	**Best Piano Solos**	$15.99
00156601	**Blessings**	$12.99
00198656	**Blues Classics**	$12.99
00284359	**Broadway Songs with a Classical Flair**	$14.99
00310669	**Broadway's Best**	$14.99
00312106	**Canzone Italiana**	$12.99
00280848	**Carpenters**	$16.99
00310629	**A Celtic Christmas**	$12.99
00310549	**The Celtic Collection**	$12.95
00280571	**Celtic Songs with a Classical Flair**	$12.99
00263362	**Charlie Brown Favorites**	$14.99
00312190	**Christmas at the Movies**	$14.99
00294754	**Christmas Carols with a Classical Flair**	$12.99
00311414	**Christmas Medleys**	$14.99
00236669	**Christmas Praise Hymns**	$12.99
00233788	**Christmas Songs for Classical Piano**	$12.99
00311769	**Christmas Worship Medleys**	$14.99
00310607	**Cinema Classics**	$15.99
00301857	**Circles**	$10.99
00311101	**Classic Wedding Songs**	$10.95
00311292	**Classical Folk**	$10.95
00311083	**Classical Jazz**	$12.95
00137779	**Coldplay for Classical Piano**	$16.99
00311103	**Contemporary Wedding Songs**	$12.99
00348788	**Country Songs with a Classical Flair**	$14.99
00249097	**Disney Recital Suites**	$17.99
00311754	**Disney Songs for Classical Piano**	$17.99
00241379	**Disney Songs for Ragtime Piano**	$17.99
00311881	**Favorite Wedding Songs**	$14.99
00315974	**Fiddlin' at the Piano**	$12.99
00311811	**The Film Score Collection**	$15.99
00269408	**Folksongs with a Classical Flair**	$12.99
00144353	**The Gershwin Collection**	$14.99
00233789	**Golden Scores**	$14.99
00144351	**Gospel Greats**	$12.99
00183566	**The Great American Songbook**	$12.99
00312084	**The Great Melodies**	$12.99
00311157	**Great Standards**	$12.95
00171621	**A Grown-Up Christmas List**	$12.99
00311071	**The Hymn Collection**	$12.99
00311349	**Hymn Medleys**	$12.99
00280705	**Hymns in a Celtic Style**	$12.99
00269407	**Hymns with a Classical Flair**	$12.99
00311249	**Hymns with a Touch of Jazz**	$12.99
00310905	**I Could Sing of Your Love Forever**	$12.95
00310762	**Jingle Jazz**	$14.99
00175310	**Billy Joel for Classical Piano**	$16.99
00126449	**Elton John for Classical Piano**	$16.99
00310839	**Let Freedom Ring!**	$12.99
00238988	**Andrew Lloyd Webber Piano Songbook**	$14.99
00313227	**Andrew Lloyd Webber Solos**	$15.99
00313523	**Mancini Magic**	$16.99
00312113	**More Disney Songs for Classical Piano**	$16.99
00311295	**Motown Hits**	$14.99
00300640	**Piano Calm**	$12.99
00339131	**Piano Calm: Christmas**	$12.99
00346009	**Piano Calm: Prayer**	$14.99
00306870	**Piazzolla Tangos**	$16.99
00156645	**Queen for Classical Piano**	$15.99
00310755	**Richard Rodgers Classics**	$16.99
00289545	**Scottish Songs**	$12.99
00310609	**Shout to the Lord!**	$14.99
00119403	**The Sound of Music**	$14.99
00311978	**The Spirituals Collection**	$10.99
00210445	**Star Wars**	$16.99
00224738	**Symphonic Hymns for Piano**	$14.99
00279673	**Tin Pan Alley**	$12.99
00312112	**Treasured Hymns for Classical Piano**	$14.99
00144926	**The Twelve Keys of Christmas**	$12.99
00278486	**The Who for Classical Piano**	$16.99
00294036	**Worship with a Touch of Jazz**	$12.99
00311911	**Yuletide Jazz**	$17.99

EASY PIANO

00210401	**Adele for Easy Classical Piano**	$15.99
00310610	**African-American Spirituals**	$10.99
00218244	**The Beatles for Easy Classical Piano**	$14.99
00218387	**Catchy Songs for Piano**	$12.99
00310973	**Celtic Dreams**	$12.99
00233686	**Christmas Carols for Easy Classical Piano**	$12.99
00311126	**Christmas Pops**	$14.99
00311548	**Classic Pop/Rock Hits**	$14.99
00310769	**A Classical Christmas**	$10.95
00310975	**Classical Movie Themes**	$12.99
00144352	**Disney Songs for Easy Classical Piano**	$12.99
00311093	**Early Rock 'n' Roll**	$14.99
00311997	**Easy Worship Medleys**	$12.99
00289547	**Duke Ellington**	$14.99
00160297	**Folksongs for Easy Classical Piano**	$12.99

00110374	**George Gershwin Classics**	$12.99
00310805	**Gospel Treasures**	$12.99
00306821	**Vince Guaraldi Collection**	$19.99
00160294	**Hymns for Easy Classical Piano**	$12.99
00310798	**Immortal Hymns**	$12.99
00311294	**Jazz Standards**	$12.99
00310744	**Love Songs**	$12.99
00233740	**The Most Beautiful Songs for Easy Classical Piano**	$12.99
00220036	**Pop Ballads**	$14.99
00311406	**Pop Gems of the 1950s**	$12.95
00311407	**Pop Gems of the 1960s**	$12.95
00233739	**Pop Standards for Easy Classical Piano**	$12.99
00102887	**A Ragtime Christmas**	$12.99
00311293	**Ragtime Classics**	$10.95
00312028	**Santa Swings**	$12.99
00233688	**Songs from Childhood for Easy Classical Piano**	$12.99
00103258	**Songs of Inspiration**	$12.99
00310840	**Sweet Land of Liberty**	$12.99
00126450	**10,000 Reasons**	$14.99
00310712	**Timeless Praise**	$12.95
00311086	**TV Themes**	$12.99
00310717	**21 Great Classics**	$12.99
00160076	**Waltzes & Polkas for Easy Classical Piano**	$12.99
00145342	**Weekly Worship**	$16.99

BIG-NOTE PIANO

00310838	**Children's Favorite Movie Songs**	$12.99
00346000	**Christmas Movie Magic**	$12.99
00277368	**Classical Favorites**	$12.99
00310907	**Contemporary Hits**	$12.99
00277370	**Disney Favorites**	$14.99
00310888	**Joy to the World**	$12.99
00310908	**The Nutcracker**	$12.99
00277371	**Star Wars**	$16.99

BEGINNING PIANO SOLOS

00311202	**Awesome God**	$12.99
00310837	**Christian Children's Favorites**	$12.99
00311117	**Christmas Traditions**	$10.99
00311250	**Easy Hymns**	$12.99
00102710	**Everlasting God**	$10.99
00311403	**Jazzy Tunes**	$10.95
00310822	**Kids' Favorites**	$12.99
00338175	**Silly Songs for Kids**	$9.99

PIANO DUET

00126452	**The Christmas Variations**	$12.99
00311350	**Classical Theme Duets**	$10.99
00295099	**Gospel Duets**	$12.99
00311544	**Hymn Duets**	$14.99
00311203	**Praise & Worship Duets**	$12.99
00294755	**Sacred Christmas Duets**	$12.99
00119405	**Star Wars**	$14.99
00253545	**Worship Songs for Two**	$12.99

Prices, contents, and availability subject to change without notice.

0221

158

CHRISTMAS COLLECTIONS
FROM HAL LEONARD
ALL BOOKS ARRANGED FOR PIANO, VOICE & GUITAR

THE BEST CHRISTMAS SONGS EVER

69 all-time favorites: Auld Lang Syne • Coventry Carol • Frosty the Snow Man • Happy Holiday • It Came Upon the Midnight Clear • O Holy Night • Rudolph the Red-Nosed Reindeer • Silver Bells • What Child Is This? • and many more.
00359130 ....$29.99

THE BIG BOOK OF CHRISTMAS SONGS

Over 120 all-time favorites and hard-to-find classics: As Each Happy Christmas • The Boar's Head Carol • Carol of the Bells • Deck the Halls • The Friendly Beasts • God Rest Ye Merry Gentlemen • Joy to the World • Masters in This Hall • O Holy Night • Story of the Shepherd • and more.
00311520 ....$22.99

CHRISTMAS SONGS – BUDGET BOOKS

100 holiday favorites: All I Want for Christmas Is You • Christmas Time Is Here • Feliz Navidad • Grandma Got Run Over by a Reindeer • I'll Be Home for Christmas • Last Christmas • O Holy Night • Please Come Home for Christmas • Rockin' Around the Christmas Tree • We Need a Little Christmas • What Child Is This? • and more.
00310887 ....$14.99

CHRISTMAS MOVIE SONGS

34 holiday hits from the big screen: All I Want for Christmas Is You • Believe • Christmas Vacation • Do You Want to Build a Snowman? • Frosty the Snow Man • Have Yourself a Merry Little Christmas • It's Beginning to Look like Christmas • Mele Kalikimaka • Rudolph the Red-Nosed Reindeer • Silver Bells • White Christmas • You're a Mean One, Mr. Grinch • and more.
00146961 ....$19.99

CHRISTMAS PIANO SONGS FOR DUMMIES®

56 favorites: Auld Lang Syne • Away in a Manger • Blue Christmas • The Christmas Song • Deck the Hall • I'll Be Home for Christmas • Jingle Bells • Joy to the World • My Favorite Things • Silent Night • more!
00311387 ....$19.95

CHRISTMAS POP STANDARDS

22 contemporary holiday hits, including: All I Want for Christmas Is You • Christmas Time Is Here • Little Saint Nick • Mary, Did You Know? • Merry Christmas, Darling • Santa Baby • Underneath the Tree • Where Are You Christmas? • and more.
00348998 ....$14.99

CHRISTMAS SING-ALONG

40 seasonal favorites: Away in a Manger • Christmas Time Is Here • Feliz Navidad • Happy Holiday • Jingle Bells • Mary, Did You Know? • O Come, All Ye Faithful • Rudolph the Red-Nosed Reindeer • Silent Night • White Christmas • and more. Includes online sing-along backing tracks.
00278176 Book/Online Audio $24.99

CHRISTMAS SONGS FOR KIDS

28 favorite songs of the season, including: Away in a Manger • Do You Want to Build a Snowman? • Here Comes Santa Claus (Right down Santa Claus Lane) • Mele Kalikimaka • Rudolph the Red-Nosed Reindeer • Santa Claus Is Comin' to Town • Silent Night • Somewhere in My Memory • and many more.
00311571 ....$12.99

100 CHRISTMAS CAROLS

Includes: Away in a Manger • Bring a Torch, Jeannette, Isabella • Coventry Carol • Deck the Hall • The First Noel • Go, Tell It on the Mountain • I Heard the Bells on Christmas Day • Joy to the World • O Come, All Ye Faithful (Adeste Fideles) • Silent Night • Sing We Now of Christmas • and more.
00310897 ....$19.99

100 MOST BEAUTIFUL CHRISTMAS SONGS

Includes: Angels We Have Heard on High • Baby, It's Cold Outside • Christmas Time Is Here • Do You Hear What I Hear • Grown-Up Christmas List • Happy Xmas (War Is Over) • I'll Be Home for Christmas • The Little Drummer Boy • Mary, Did You Know? • O Holy Night • White Christmas • Winter Wonderland • and more.
00237285 ....$24.99

POPULAR CHRISTMAS SHEET MUSIC: 1980-2017

40 recent seasonal favorites: All I Want for Christmas Is You • Because It's Christmas (For All the Children) • Breath of Heaven (Mary's Song) • Christmas Lights • The Christmas Shoes • The Gift • Grown-Up Christmas List • Last Christmas • Santa Tell Me • Snowman • Where Are You Christmas? • Wrapped in Red • and more.
00278089 ....$17.99

A SENTIMENTAL CHRISTMAS BOOK

27 beloved Christmas favorites, including: The Christmas Shoes • The Christmas Song (Chestnuts Roasting on an Open Fire) • Christmas Time Is Here • Grown-Up Christmas List • Have Yourself a Merry Little Christmas • I'll Be Home for Christmas • Somewhere in My Memory • Where Are You Christmas? • and more.
00236830 ....$14.99

ULTIMATE CHRISTMAS

100 seasonal favorites: Auld Lang Syne • Bring a Torch, Jeannette, Isabella • Carol of the Bells • The Chipmunk Song • Christmas Time Is Here • The First Noel • Frosty the Snow Man • Gesù Bambino • Happy Holiday • Happy Xmas (War Is Over) • Jingle-Bell Rock • Pretty Paper • Silver Bells • Suzy Snowflake • and more.
00361399 ....$24.99

A VERY MERRY CHRISTMAS

39 familiar favorites: Blue Christmas • Feliz Navidad • Happy Xmas (War Is Over) • I'll Be Home for Christmas • Jingle-Bell Rock • Please Come Home for Christmas • Rockin' Around the Christmas Tree • Santa, Bring My Baby Back (To Me) • Sleigh Ride • White Christmas • and more.
00310536 ....$14.99